The Epidemic of Marketing Fear

Red Affairs, Blue Prescriptions, and Faith Dispositions

Cuffee the Magnificent

CUFFEE MEDIA GROUP

DEDICATION

This is dedicated to risk takers, innovators, fear slayers, and indigo children. Create life.

CONTENTS

1. TRIANGLE

The universal egg is the infinite becoming finite, through a process

So we wrap innovation and creativity, like bacon, around perpetual progress

With this soda machine, how can we simply push products and be satisfied?

How can we provide mediocre services and call it certified?

The institutions of fear say that happiness is for the after hour drive

Sit down, shut up, and be mechanical if you want to survive

Even the so-called glory of entrepreneurship is abstract

Driven by how much profit can be made rather than impact

Satisfying demand and fulfilling orders is the lifestyle

But my sixth sense challenges me to go 180 miles

They glorify ignorance as the pathway to millions

They depict luxury as the pinnacle for civilians

They speak of retirement and so-called financial freedom, like ecstasy

But what is freedom compared to the glory of legacy and destiny?

Does a warrior want liberty or the glory that is greater?

Does an emperor want to be free or upheld as a savior?

Empowered for destiny and purpose is true liberty

Not to be free from everything, but to have your name in liturgy

Empowered to be an attendee at the black tie ballet

How can we take the light of truth and hide it away?

Just one more advertisement to create an earthquake

One more sales call for my quota to make

We say forget friendship, because I'm trying to make money

But the great surprise is that there is no milk and honey

Cuffee magic at the foundation makes a tower eternal

Babel was evil because it's purpose was not maternal

Rise above the clouds not for accumulation, but for the story

Have not the hands of a hoarder, but the hands of glory

The ax is at the root and if the tree is a facade it will fall

The river is wide and the flood is a stream of ethanol

With blue prescriptions, the foundation is tested

But with red affairs, your castle will be manifested

2. AFFAIR

What is the prevailing ideology that guides organizations?

It is the ideology of fear and it's many persuasions

It is false evidence appearing real, and without question we believe

And we fear every ounce of it, without proof to receive

It is the master of the business world and it keeps us from risk

The risk that is so necessary to save glory on a hard disk

We must leap into the infinite default template of passion and brisk

And believe with confidence, rather than infringe upon a frisk

Our society is built on fear, and our leaders lead with terror in heart

Making false evidence that appears real in every part

Their rule seems absolute in the present state of human knowledge

Because it is based upon having affairs with shadows after college

The horror and pain of what is expected, if you drink it

Our whole life is wrapped in it like a newborn blanket

The most important subject of human life is in a backward state

We move forward, just a little, but yet afraid to participate

We abandoned the cave and entered marketing, yet we are still lost

Our sales atmosphere walks aimlessly with big minds to defrost

Yet our large temples lead us neither to clarity or religious cost

Our morality is garbage and we imagine the worst before the best

Even the so-called greatest among us are without behest

But there are those of us that still exist even now in truth

Yes, we are held captive in schools of old thinking with youth

We are at war against ourselves, because we know the system is wrong

We have false memories of submission to a pledge and a song

After 5,000 years of debate, the same line continues on and on

That the troublemakers among us are the geniuses to add on

But fear prevents the unity of purpose among visionaries and lieutenants

Our philosophies are under the same contending banner of helots

Our mission is not to think for people about their futures unknown

The blind world keeps us from making the unknown known

But greatness is our mission, from within to without

We do not merely seek to accumulate profits from doubt

We are living by giving with a utilitarian humanity

Our ambition is toward an infinite spirituality

Continuous progress toward what is good and harmonious

Spreading truth throughout the world and making light victorious

But many of us are too afraid to leave the darkness and take a chance

We are so familiar with death that we are horrified by dance

We are so in love with mere survival and destruction that we run from love

We are so familiar with comparisons that we are burned from above

Let our mission not be one of metal weights and balances through

But of immeasurable quality and beauty, not prescriptions blue

3. TALENT

Defy fear in yourself and follow your intuition

The process of selling should not be superstition

When fishing for cats, I don't think about what I'm wanting

I think about what they are corresponding

I don't bait the hook with strawberries and ice cream

Rather, I dangle a worm or a grasshopper in the water stream

Why not use this common sense when fishing for people?

Why are we so selfish, childish, and feeble?

Of course, you are eternally interested in what you want

Even interested in dating alone in a restaurant

We used to be just like you, full of doubt

Stop trying to have one foot in and one foot out

Help others by talking about what they want, first

Then tell them of the truth that you have rehearsed

Jump in, stop selling, and start sharing what is true

Stop marketing and start sharing Mountain Dew

The question is, what are you eagerly wanting?

What service can you render before departing?

Defy fear and help us destroy this ideology that plagues us

Our society needs champions that we can trust

Actions come from what we fundamentally desire

In business and in life we must aspire for something higher

Destroy this ideology that plagues our society

Meditate only on limitless possibility

4. DESIGN

Our visions exist because we believe the global financier

The world we live in is guided by the ideology of fear

So how can our mission be a vision of the illiterate?

How can our goals be S.M.A.R.T. and also ignorant?

I declare, dare to do the impossible and fear what is pleasant

Discomfort is the best comfort when hierarchies are present

They baptize supervisors that use fear and terror

But don't be a "better to be feared than loved" wearer

Rather, embrace the wisdom found in compassion

It is better to be a distributor of human rights and passion

Specific, because we are infinite in this game of scrabble

Measurable, because it comes from the immovable

Attainable, because nothing is impossible

Relevant, because all things are probable

Timely, because revolutions have time zones

So we must liquidate our goals and milestones

Will we manifest our fears of being homeless?

Will we drink at the bar of the doubtful and hopeless?

Limitation is our handicapping agent

How many people can we reach with a potential latent?

How much can our revenue grow without accounting?

How many triple balance sheets are we mounting?

Are titans destined to be bound forever to one mountain?

Are immortal-mortals destined to be chained to a fountain?

Innovation and creativity throughout the solar system is what we strive

Expressing limitless possibilities is how we thrive

How many Youtube views should you have in one day?

Perhaps the day-to-day grind of sales transactions can keep you at bay?

Perhaps the paralysis of analysis is keeping you alive?

Perhaps your financial statements can survive smooth stones of five?

The slingshot helps us look up and never look to

Lift up your heads and look to the infinite through

The immeasurable and the indescribable kingdom advance

We seek the destiny of raindrops in the ocean of the expanse

5. PASSION

It's autumn in new york, so stop seeking profits

Seek greatness with illuminated deposits

Stop seeking financial success in this season

Start seeking your destiny and purpose with cohesion

The call upon your life will be discovered with intuition

The path you will take will be found in prayer and meditation

Childish and impulsive people guide many

So we need risk-takers and intuitive geniuses plenty

As an integral part of every business and every profession

The climate is now that solutions are needed for progression

There is no choice but to seek innovation and creativity

Compassion is the greatest of success, yet we place it in captivity

Show the strength of humility over our doubts and fears

Move the goal post from quantitative to qualitative pioneers

In business school, they taught me to use S.M.A.R.T. goals

But intuition makes our smart goals look like buttonholes

Greatness requires passion and desire

Inspiration must inhabit the vessel's fire

Greatness can't come from arbitrary numbers on a board

Fulfillment can't be measured like the beauty of a minor chord

Success comes from a destiny harpsichord

Victory comes from a glory storyboard

The climate is on the side of light

The climate is changing and continues to underwrite

The climate will soon be the brightness of upright

The climate will be fearless forever if we expedite

Innovation is infinite in measure

Creativity will end never

Seek the truth hidden in the foundation

Meditate on how to spread light through this space station

6. SHAPE

Now is the time to leave the neutral zone and make a choice

If you do not choose, you will be erased from history's voice

Like snow in Tokyo, the land of apathy is now fading

Vaccines of polio, prevent the epidemic from parading

Usually the easiest option is the first to take

But we have an opportunity to fight the invisible snake

We can meet on the field of battle for glory sake

But fear makes us cowards in the face of our biggest break

Choose this day whom you will serve, ignorance or glory

Do you want to be a footnote or have a legacy and epic story

Innovation is not something that just happens without causation

It is the chain reaction of nuclear fusion in an explosion of concentration

If you look through history, past and future, for innovation

You will find that it is a result of following one's passion and obsession

It is a choice to focus on quality and not cheap tinker toys

Because, we need no more quick fixes and temporary joys

Rather, we need happiness with utilitarian products and services

Social enterprises with sustainability that always resurfaces

Filled with righteous indignation, we choose to add value to the market

We don't need false evidence appearing real as a narcotic

Our schools of thought should not be filled with fluff to pacify

Rather, it should be wholesome, filled with micronutrients to oversupply

If the product is crap then it deserves to be exposed as a lie

As a salesperson your duty is to let that evil products die

Make a decision today to be a force for good and expose the bait

How can we be of integrity if we peddle diseases to create?

If the service is terrible then it deserves to fail

It's not just a metaphysical ethic, it is the Robin Hood tale

The universal principle is the manifestation of beauty on the screen

As entrepreneurs and salespeople we should not degrade caffeine

We can be a vending machine of ignorance to the pedestrian

Or we can operate by faith and business, as a utilitarian

We can be gatekeepers of light, and uphold the canon of a market quality

Please remember, we aren't here just to make money

When you use intuition, you see that we occupy the stars

A global transformation of entrepreneurs to blue avatars

A whole new world of creativity is what we seek

So be convicted and contribute to the social critique

Citizens of the world awaken and see that inside you is a seed

Take your place not as a peddler of trinkets, but have a title deed

Joint heirs with compassion through a business enterprise

Choose ye this day to be a warrior of light when post-scarcity is authorized

7. COLOR

But when I follow the intuition inside, it leads me away from manipulation

Like a piece of pie it leads me from deception to meditation

The difficulty is not avoiding the popularity of natural faults in humanity

But challenging ourselves not to conquer and seek every penny

We still dispute if we should follow our intuition out of the Matrix

Because we were taught to abandon right and wrong and be lunatics

Our primary senses of sight and sound determine what is real

So with the proper illusion someone can be tricked to feel

So we steal and take what we want from the masses

Calling them sheep and cattle in a game of fishing classes

We assume that our selling techniques will help us rule

We assume that our persuasion is our fated spool

But this leads me to shout out to my customers and clients

Defy fear! Defy it at any cost because you are giants!

The world should look up to you for what is possible

Not to people who live in the concrete probable

For we believe that nothing is impossible

The intuitive says that all consumer demand is solvable

The prevailing system of the world has general laws

They are presented as questions that cause us to pause

What if things don't work out, and we fail?

What if everything I've built is to no avail?

Am I even able to accomplish anything at all?

What if I am a waste of space after all?

The intuitive person takes a risk because greatness is in her long view

Destiny and vision can be accomplished with straightness to pursue

The intuitive person brings light to your purchasing power

And she does it because compassion is her tower

Let the meaning of these terms be understood

We must expose the lies of manipulation and forsake livelihood

Like a piece of pie, we do not calculate our lives

Like a piece of pie, our ventures should seek to serve our afterlives

Fear will no longer hold us from our greatness

The red carpet is laid for our fashionable lateness

8. DECOR

We, as entrepreneurs and leaders, are stuck in this vortex of fear

Manipulation and deception on the surface of the black sphere

Urban trends forecast that the weather will be four seasons

Urban trends predict the termination of all reasons

Urban trends reveal the worthlessness of our conclusions

Urban trends are apparitions of nuclear fusions

Concerning the description of KFC as an anomaly

I was taught to simply pass go, when creating a monopoly

The doctrines of science are not usually spoon fed to us

Nor do they usually have the evidence thrust upon us

Even in sales training, one of the tenants of selling is to use fear of loss

It is even called the first principle in colors of the cross

If it wasn't true, then there would be no scientific method to study

Life was considerably easy when banks were consistently plenty

We were unaware that we were poor, and had nothing

If you want a customer to behave, then tell them they will lose something

They will pull out credit cards and rush to buy anything

Because our British law dictates that fear is the king of everything

It is indeed a mystery of mysteries that evicts our theology

It is accepted as a fundamental law of consumer psychology

In sales and marketing we use fear as a tool of manipulation

We are told that it is the metaphysics of stimulation

The elementary school of philosophy was converted

But Maslow and Freud are still apostles among the introverted

Their relationship to science is not that of a foundation edified

We are trained to use fear in leadership, and it is justified

Niccolo is Moses, with fear as the greatest of all stone tablets

Like a scroll coming from Mount Olympus down to Atlas

But at the root of the tree I challenge this so-called business of heaven

I say that light will expose this false belief from Seven to Devin

In the art of sales, the hypothesis precedes the theory

The contrary might be expected when asking Siri

I've done it! I've successfully brought legislation to morality!

Will you defy fear with me, and have an entrepreneurial spirituality?

Urban trends project that all actions are for the sake of some end

Urban trends seem to illustrate that holistic marketing will ascend

Urban trends lead us in a pursuit of truth and light in sales

Urban trends defeat the status quo that money and profit prevails

9. DRAMA

When you follow your intuition in business, it will open your awareness

It will direct you to the land of justice and fairness

Therefore, we must bring a halt to isolation and alienation

We must follow the voice from Zion to an alien nation

What is the 100 year vision of the prospect you are targeting?

Who is the leader of the prospect you are harvesting?

Can you qualify the lead based on love and compassion?

Are they spiritually mature enough to handle your fashion?

Do they have the wisdom to properly apply your services?

Is their unity among ranks or is chaos the king of surfaces?

Salespeople need questions like these to be guided by

Review the feed to see if the lead is even qualified

He that wins customers is wise and gains honor

One should seek death before manipulating with dishonor

Leaders are needed to spread light throughout the market

Salespeople are needed to file the truth on the docket

Write holistic and comprehensive formulas for profit

Only if it is good for my home and my tribe, then composite

If you live only for profit then your goods are in the out-house

This is not a call to console with flowers and a casket blouse

This is a challenge to be accepted or rejected

Light does not ask permission from darkness to run unrestricted

Light stands on the scene and ignorance has no choice but to tower

Like a coward it will flee and even be devoured

We need premium quality and innovations

We need perpetual improvements and creative solutions

With light in the market, darkness can not comprehend

The blind and deaf can't see, hear, or even defend

Not until eyes are opened and ears are unplugged

Not until evidence disproves Atlas Shrugged

Intuition is truth, objective and subjective, in nature

The cold steel of subliminal messages, a falling elevator

Aspiring entrepreneurs look to the ancient and old

But the future belongs to those that proliferate light reflecting gold

10. PRESCRIPTION

But why? Why don't we do this venture for right?

Because we are afraid to edit and rewrite?

We speak of lofty goals of attainment but don't even care

Our customers are in a database as numbers to spare

We love to speak of the ills and failures of others

But the old contact lenses in our eyes are dry shutters

The milestones must be short and long with a choice between

We can have a holistic view on life, as one to dream

We, as entrepreneurs and leaders, are afraid that we will fail

But if we follow our hearts then we will prevail

We must choose to accept or reject what is good for all humanity

I recommend whatever is fair, free, and full of veracity

We are afraid and fearful of everything that lurks in the shadows

So we don't do the right thing, we try to control all commandos

Our mission in business is to accept the formula or reject it

We can believe that darkness and fear is the key or we can correct it

Overcoming fear is the chief obstacle which keeps us from genuine wealth

So we end up not doing what is best for humanity and global commonwealth

We take the easy road and do what everybody else does

We seek profit first, and profit alone, by creating a buzz

We comfort our selfishness by giving to charity with fanfare

But the gross misconception is that PR stunts are malware

Simplify everything and remove the chains of professional peer pressure

Enter the philosophy of giving and receiving the title of professor

Concerning the utilitarian standard, illustrations create the doctrine

The view shows me more clearly the governance of the sovereign

What good is giving to charity if you are contributing to an evil system

A system of fear and doubt filled with worry and skepticism

I shall prepare to throw more light at this question

The mission should involve intuition at the reception

You are contributing to the problem by being a fear distributor

Forget judging drug dealers, when we are death dealers

If you are not following your intuition, then we are concealer

It is false evidence appearing real, and we believe it without proof

Like rats in a cage, drowning in waterproof

The troublemakers among us are the geniuses we need

But fear prevents the unity of visionaries and lieutenants to lead

Meditate on mankind at large and it's future stampede

Dedicate your life again to quality and beauty indeed

11. MOTHER

As an entrepreneur and organizational leader

Follow your intuition when printing your employee reader

It will challenge everything society tells you

But the one who thinks of victory while arising from HQ, will subdue

Before engaging in battle, one must seek strategic factors

Without calculations there are only tactical subtractors

If you have many knights and bishops, you have many favors and flavors

Marketing intuition seeks greatness not profit slavers

Be the servant of all stakeholders, not just shareholders

We will win if we have more strategic factors, not leftovers

How can they win if they have no strategic factors?

So I prophesy that we will conquer the reactors

The greatest one is the servant of all in our digital organization

Blessed are the poor, meek, merciful, and pure in search optimization

And blessed are those that are persecuted for doing the right thing

Because there is only one way under heaven to get anyone to do anything

Team leaders are the primary way to make the other into a brother

Team leaders have the key and you can't find another

Team leaders, you will conclude, when you follow sales intuition

Team leaders help you defy fear and have a spirit of creative ambition

She will lead you in the direction of fulfilling your purpose in life

If she threatens you with a revolver in your ribs before the afterlife

You can't force your employees to give you cooperation

Until their back is threatened with fire in their imagination

You can't force a child to be obedient with bruises and elevations

Because they have unexpected consequences and mobilizations

Rather, trade in your ideology of fear for the faith disposition

The only way I can get you to do anything is to buy your tuition

Your desire to be important reminds me of the importance of a microwave

What do you want to do? What do you crave?

Team leaders challenge their people to embrace the grave

Team leaders lead you away from merely selling a service

She will lead you away from marketing to a righteous nervous

The higher call to spread light throughout the world is braver

Strategic factors from intuition is in her favor

There are better ways than simply pushing products in a booth

It will lead you toward the greater call to teach and share the truth

Meditation will lead you away from simply marketing variety

And lead you to the higher call of spreading light throughout society

12. CREATION

When entrepreneurs and sales professionals are texting

Follow your intuition when operating is everything

As an entrepreneur, you need a sales machine to establish and grow

As a professional, you need a sales animal, like an impresario

Hire a machine to recruit and fundraise, like a fireball

Sales intuition seeks greatness as a servant of all

Be a servant of all stakeholders, not just shareholders

And all stakeholders should be carryovers

Because blessed are the poor, meek, merciful, and pure in heart

Meditation for those persecuted will soon start

Meditation for defying fear will see a tortoise speak

Are you reading this book to find a new marketing technique?

Are you trying to win friends with black coffee, unsweetened?

Are you trying to influence people by selling a mutual fund?

That's like an extraterrestrial with a blade, but without a knife

That will not help you fulfill your purpose in life

And you know what's really behind this reality tv show

Effects and defects with ulterior motives in the audio

He wants to sell you something that you have to undo

Real estate, eminent domain, and not to marry you

Do I know this from some divine instinct or petition?

Did I learn it from the ideology of fear or a faith disposition?

Test it out by being genuinely interested in people for two years

Reprogram your collective consciousness as social engineers

If you gain an interest, then you'll meet what you make

You'll make more friends in two months than you can take

Far more made in two years, than if centered on you

It will lead you away from pushing products away from you

You will be a magnet of people as sister and brother

And people will accept the other as if introduced by a mother

Of course, it doesn't work when you live under the sea

As a mermaid, how can you not be interested in me?

Interested only in yourself, all morning, noon, and dinner

But it's time to stop marketing and become a red pill winner

Answer the higher call to Zion, which we did discuss

End the preoccupation with having people interested in us

We will never have a crowded feast of sincere close friends

Because friends, real friends, are not tied strings but burnt ends

The individual with external interests is the greatest

The hardship playlist is on repeat, forget the latest

It is from among such individuals that all human failures spring

It is from among such individuals we innovate and create everything

13. SUCCESS

Mechanical inputs and outputs can't produce a royal fedora

We praise the assembly line like the words of the Torah

But what can compare to the indescribable metrics of handiwork

The element that makes it efficient is lost in translation

Rather, use your intuition when running your organization

You will question everything that the textbook said was imperial

Start the startup with passion even if your profit is a bowl of cereal

Sell the best solution and quit your job to heal

Make a lasting impact and welcome to the land of the real

Publicity isn't really charity if it's a stunt to create perception

You are robbing from the light givers and perpetuating deception

All warfare is not deception, all warfare is intuition

Because the universal principle is universal ambition

Sales intuition says to seek greatness not profit

If you fail, then fall as a graceful prophet

If you die, then die with a dignified respiratory

If you lose everything, then go down with flames of glory

The race is not to win

The battle is not the winners to begin

The competition is not for the gold medal

Rather, create life and pollinate the ambrosia pedal

The challenge is to create life within the corners of four

Yes, it has always been about a world tour

Effectiveness? I say, let it burn clean

Efficiency? I say, let it turn pale and mold green

Bottlenecks and gap assessments don't require videoconferencing

For we are not seeking perfection in sales and marketing

We seek greatness, and the greatest is the servant of all

To be the servant of all we have to fall

We serve the community that was and wasn't executed

Because blessed are the pure in heart that are persecuted

Are we telling the truth and spreading light wholly?

If we are, then seek intuition and courage, the one and only

14. ANSWER

The quarterly earnings call is a killer

Taking innovation and creativity from the caterpillar

It is the assassin of world changing animals and adults

Why should we exchange our destiny for quick results?

Arriba and abajo, it continues expressively

Business cycles abound before the end of scarcity

Economic troughs feed the pigs like a periodical

But, is that what life is all about in biological?

Is sales all about creating lists and drafting a graphic?

Is marketing all about inbound and outbound traffic?

Is profit the only purpose of the entrepreneurial key?

Is the dry stale rice cakes of transactions all there is to be?

If so, then I want nothing to do with the garbage collected

Where are the woods, so I can join the wolf pack connected?

But if we take the long view with milestones incrementally

The finite comes from the infinite and a child is born instrumentally

Your destiny is immeasurable but it will be manifested in a missionary

It will takes a group of people brought together by a visionary

A vision to make a great grand impact

A vision that has every inch intact

A vision that seems impossible to the current marketplace

If it doesn't dare to do the impossible, then it is a disgrace

Wake up the disposition of faith inside you by amending

Believe first, then have the track repeat unending

See it and feel it, brand new every morning

Dream a dream and never let it stop warming

The expectation of quick results discourages

But the infinite vision with infinite milestones encourages

No matter what happens I'm pressing toward equality

Take action to produce immortality and a godly quality

Not for short-term results but for long-term success

Not for just a few old cults but until all confess

That wealth doesn't rain in a passing cloud

But found in the bacteria of the composting shroud

15. FASHION

A guide can lead tourists to the island's false superiority

Or the interior where it's dirty, smelly, and full of poverty

The facade perpetuates the ignorance that's towering

But the truth about the mud between our toes is not empowering

Deception is the name of the game with workshop facilitators

The blissfulness of sales gurus is that they are master manipulators

But a piece of your soul must be exchanged for their motivation

But those of us with a sixth sense want meat in our education

Yes, it is true, intuitive people see the wealth in things eternal

So with this, we say that the best way is to defy fear with our fraternal

Yes, it is true, we have a spirit of entrepreneurship

And the risk is well worth it, because you will take ownership

The risk of failure can't compare to the gold produced inside you

You see? Fear of failure makes you lose revenue

It leaves you disabled, so you can't begin

But genuine wealth and richness are therein

Where can I find a billion dollars? It's within

Where can I find a trillion dollars? You can find it herein

You can find wealth untold within a silhouette

You say, my bills, my rent, my utilities, and my debt?

My response to you is, what about your destiny?

What about your purpose in life, and your identity?

Let your intuition lead you away from living by the ideology

Let it lead you away from pushing theology and mythology

The best way is to be led by a greater call, by targeting

Go above and beyond simple-minded marketing

Hear the higher call of spreading light throughout the world's drills

Let the bills worry about the bills

Let the utility worry about the utility

The debt will flee from your tranquility

Keep your eyes on the prize of victory

Bonfires and war paint, while telling the story of your glory

ABOUT THE AUTHOR

Cuffee the Magnificent? Who is he?
Musician, poet, and promoter of innovation and creativity
Passion for life and truth to bring the show
Supported by Cuffee Media Group, to let the people know
The revolution will be improvised
The gifts will be exercised
The flourishing of innovation in society
Follow you dreams and explore our creativity
Limitless, so dare to do the impossible
Risk takers, because nothing is impossible
Defy fear and take ownership
Defy fear and have a spirit of entrepreneurship

www.ingramcontent.com/pod-product-compliance
Lightning Source LLC
Chambersburg PA
CBHW032021190326
41520CB00007B/575